# The Hawaiian Chronicles – Our Hawaiian Cruise Adventures

## A Travel Guide About a Hawaiian Journey

### Travels Across America Series – Volume II

# Paul R. Wonning

The Hawaiian Chronicles – Our Hawaiian Adventures

The Hawaiian Chronicles – Our Hawaiian Cruise Adventures

Published Paul R. Wonning

Copyright 2014 by Paul R. Wonning

Print Edition



If you would like email notification of when new installments of

this series are available, email the author for inclusion in the subscription list.

Paul R. Wonning

paulwonning@gmail.com

Facebook Mossy Feet Books

**Mossy Feet Books**

## Description

*The Hawaiian Chronicles – Our Hawaiian Adventures* serves as both a journal of our Hawaiian cruise adventure and as a guide of the various types of cruises available for visitors to tour our 50th State. It is possible for vacationers to tour all of the major islands on a single, seven-day journey. This guide does not attempt to cover all of the destination to visit on the islands. *The Hawaiian Chronicles – Our Hawaiian Adventures* lists the major cruise lines and the types of cruises they offer. Contact information for the cruise lines is included in the book.

## Table of Contents

Paul R. Wonning

# The Hawaiian Chronicles – Our Hawaiian Adventures
## Episode I - The Journey Begins

### Richard Paul

To celebrate our 25th wedding anniversary the wife and I ventured to our 50th state. Many hours of planning and deliberation went into this journey. Our first debates centered on the method of transportation. I wanted to drive while the wife felt an airplane might be better. Much discussion centered on this controversy, and I am chagrined to admit I finally had to relent. Hours of research led me to believe that there is no highway to Hawaii, a serious omission on the part of our road builders. No road, no car! The wife was right, we had to fly.

So now that we had determined our mode of travel, what to do upon arrival? The wife wanted to sightsee! You know, actually drive around and look at things! Just like a couple of tourists. My idea was to hang out at the beach and look cool, just like they do on Baywatch. The wife made some snide remarks about my unique physique. The remarks intimated that it was not conducive to looking cool on the beach, which led to more discussions. Our negotiations soon centered on a cruise or a dogsled tour. The wife seemed to think that there weren't any dogsleds on Hawaii, so the Hawaiian Cruise won out.

We would tour the Hawaiian Islands aboard the ship SS Independence of the American Cruise Lines. The tour would include four islands and five ports in seven days. Beginning on Maui in the port of Kahalui on Sunday the ship would proceed to the port of Hilo on the island of Hawaii, the Big Island. We would spend Monday in Hilo. It would then proceed to the Kona Coast port of Kailua on Tuesday. Wednesday and Thursday, we would spend on the island of Oahu in the port of Honolulu. Friday's destination would be Nawilili on the island of Kauai. Saturday we would return to Maui

for the flight home.

The AAA travel agency in Columbus, Indiana handled our travel arrangements.  Our itinerary included:

Cincinnati

Ohio

Dallas

Texas

Los Angeles

California

Honolulu

Hawaii

Kahalui

Packing and other preparatory arrangements were a nightmare. The wife wanted to pack scads of clothing. I said, hell, everyone in Hawaii walks around in swimming trunks and flip-flops, we don't need any clothes. She said I been to too many Jimmy Buffet concerts, which led to more discussions. Which I lost. Again. In the weeks before departure, the wife was in a frenzy of activity - shopping and picking out clothes to take. There were clothes hanging all over the house. They hung on doors, chairs, and chandeliers. Shoot, I went to sleep watching a basketball game and awoke to find six pairs of pants and some shirts hanging from my big toe. On the day of departure, we had twenty-five suitcases, six duffels, three backpacks, her purse and my wallet. I said this seemed a little extreme as we only had two backs, how could we use three backpacks. I actually won this point! EEEhah!

The day of our departure finally arrived on February 17, 2001. Our initial flight was out of Cincinnati, Ohio on Comair Flight 6009 to Dallas, Texas at 7:00 AM. Anyone that flies a lot probably hates it. However, this was only my second flight by commercial airline and I thoroughly enjoyed the experience. We have done a fair amount of traveling, but always by car. The take off was smooth, the sunrise above the clouds just spectacular. I am amazed at how hard the flight attendants work rolling the cart up and down the aisle - always with a smile. We arrived above Dallas about 9:30, landing at 9:45. This is, as all times will be for the flight out, Indiana Time. Dallas looks nice from the air. There must have been heavy rains as the rivers and streams looked flooded. We breakfasted at the airport, and then departed Dallas at 11:25 AM for Los Angeles on Delta Flight 2119. I had a window seat so I had a good view of the landscape underneath until we got to the Rockies. Since clouds now obscured the view, we passed the time reading.

Arrival in LA was around 2:30 PM. Here we had a rather lengthy layover so we ate, read, and slept. We finally boarded the plane for Hawaii at 5:45 PM. Delta Flight 1579 left LA at 6:15 PM for Honolulu, Hawaii. The view of the receding California coast was the last thing we would see for a while, as the sky over the Pacific was mostly cloudy. Seeing the mainland slip away was both exciting and scary.

When the plane began its descent to the islands, it was about 11:30 PM Indiana time. This is about 6:30 PM Hawaii time, so it was still daylight. We passed over the island of Oahu and started our approach to Honolulu International Airport. Honolulu is impressive from the air at night. The city is lit up above the sparkling Pacific waters. The volcanic mountains constitute a striking backdrop. It is a beautiful sight.

Although we were flying on the same plane from Honolulu to Kahului, we had to leave the plane so they could clean it. I told the flight attendants that the wife enjoyed cleaning. Would the consider a discount on the far if she vacuumed while I finished my nap? While the attendant considered this request, my shin developed a rather sharp pain. Needles to say, we left the plane. The flight crew noticed my limp.

We departed Honolulu for Kahului at about 1:00 AM. It was completely dark now, so we could see nothing of the island below us except lights. All our flights that day had been smooth, so the flight from Honolulu to Kahluiu was memorable for its uniqueness. The plane passed over two mountain ranges, and I swear the plane hit every mountain in them both. Moreover, they didn't fully pressurize the plane's cabin. My head felt like an over inflated basketball on the way up, and like the inside of a flushed toilet on the way down.

We landed at Kahului at 1:30 AM (Indiana Time) - 8:30 PM Hawaii time. Representatives of the American Hawaiian Cruise line met us at the airport. They collected our luggage, which by this time was in much better shape than we were. They herded us on a bus and took us to the port for check-in. Here another representative of the Line greeted us. By this time, my head felt like someone had stuck it in a jug, sucked out all the air, and then smashed the jug with a hammer. OOOh the joys of air travel. By 2:00 AM, nineteen hours after leaving winter in Indiana, we were in the tropics! The Cruise Line had a special lunch prepared for arrivals. We ate, found our way back to our stateroom somehow, and immediately fell asleep. Welcome to Hawaii!

**NOTE:** *This trip occurred in 2001. Sadly, the American Cruise Lines has gone out of business and the SS Independence to the scrap heap.*

## The Hawaiian Chronicles
## Episode II - Maui

Upon awakening the next morning, I discovered the meaning of the term 'jet lag'. As I came to, I realized my body had achieved a rare phenomenon - multiple states of existence. My head and body were in different time zones. As I attempted to move my limbs, I realized further that not all my body parts were in the same zone. Some were in Indiana yet. Others were in Texas. More had stayed in California. None was in Hawaii. My head ached.

My attitude at the moment was," OK, we're here now. So what"? Our frenzied pace from the day before left stark impressions. Our dark arrival and the Spartan appearance of the buildings were not very Hawaii-like. We had walked out on deck briefly after eating, but we couldn't see anything in the dark.

Then there was the cabin. Don't get me wrong, the cabin was clean and smelled good. But it was small. Quite small. The bed was also small, but it did have a good mattress that promised a good night's sleep. Put these little things all together, and they dulled our anticipation. Based on what we had experienced so far, we could have been in Ohio.

After arising, I dressed, (sort of) and went searching for coffee. Somehow, I negotiated the maze of corridors and elevators to the Ohana Lounge, seeking breakfast. I let my nose lead me to the coffee. I had read in the brochures that only they would serve only coffee from the Kona Coast of Hawaii on the ship. I am no connoisseur of coffee, but the stuff, when I tasted it, was delicious.

Noticing that the room opened on to the rear deck of the ship, and that it was now daylight, I thought I would get my first real view of Hawaii. I wandered on deck in a glum, headachy mood.

First, a bit of geography. The shape of Maui is sort of like a dumbbell. Several volcanic peaks populate the west side of the island. These are the West Maui Mountains and the 'iao Valley bisects them. Please, do not ever ask me to pronounce this name. It is beautiful in Hawaiian, but when I try to say it, it sounds like I have a bug in my throat.

The east side of the island is much larger than the west side. The 8,201-foot peak of Mt. Haleakala dominates it. The ship was in port at Kahului. Located on the north end of the coastal valley that occupies the narrow part of the island, it is a pretty city. It was the lovely 'iao Valley that first met my eyes as I came on deck. The early morning sun illuminated the mists rising out of the tropical forest that covered the volcanic peaks. This is one of the most stirring sights I have ever seen. Then I turned to the left and saw the massive peak of Mt. Haleakala. Snow covered, stark, and huge, it contrasted with the tropical scene to the west.

I forgot the jet lag and headache in an instant.

I hurried to the cabin to fetch Lynne. She had been rather ho-hum about the situation too.

Together we went on deck. By now it was lighter than when I was there earlier, so the view was even more stunning. It began to dawn on us that yes, we really were in Hawaii, not Ohio. We had to tear our selves away from this enchanting scene to eat breakfast. The ship would remain in port until 2:00 PM, so we would have time to do a little sightseeing. We had signed up for a guided tour of the 'iao Valley and Tropical Plantation. The tour left the ship at 8:30, so we had to hustle through our breakfast on deck.

The tour wound up a beautiful mountain road to 'iao Valley Park. Here we marveled at the wonderful view of the 'iao Needle to the southwest and the fabulous view of the ocean back to the north. The scenery on this road rather resembles the area of the Great Smoky Mountains, if you don't look too close at the vegetation.

Upon arrival at the park, the guide told us to enjoy the park; we would be on our own for about half an hour. We wandered around the various trails of this beautiful park. A stream tumbled and cascaded down through this valley. Tropical plants bloomed, and the morning was fragrant with the misty mountain air.

With reluctance, we returned to the bus, and continued down the road. Winding back down the valley, we stopped at the Kepaniwai Park. This park features four different types of tropical gardens - Japanese, Hawaiian, Chinese, and Philippine. The most striking item here was a huge banyan tree.

The next stop on the tour was at the Tropical Plantation, which is a working plantation that grows a variety of tropical crops. The Plantation is a tourist destination featuring guided tram tours of the plantation. Coconut, pineapple, sugar cane, ginger, and coffee are just some of the crops grown here. A gift shop on the premises sells many of their products, some local Hawaiian goods, and some 'touristy' stuff. We bought a couple of souvenirs and returned to the bus. Overall, it was a first class operation.

We were back at the boat by 1:00 PM, in time for lunch at the copiously stocked Ohana Buffet. We ate on deck as the ship shoved off. The tug that pushed us out of the harbor followed along beside for a while.

We attended a mandatory 'fire drill' at 1:45, which took about half an hour. The information here would have been useful if the ship had decided to imitate the Titanic. Happily, we didn't need the practice we received.

The boat took the long way from Kahului to Hilo, passing between the islands of Maui and Molokai, Lanai, and Kahoolawe. These islands are all close enough to be visible from Maui. At one time, we could see as many as three islands at one time. In this stretch of ocean, we sighted many whales in the waters between the islands, spouting and cavorting in the waves.

We were both somewhat worried about seasickness, and when the ship hit open ocean we found out what the term 'sea legs' means. The weather was windy and the waves were high. The ship pitched and rolled. I got a little bit of a 'queasy' feeling for an hour or so, which passed and never came back. Lynne had an uneasy 'butterflies' sensation when the ship was rocking' and rolling' for the first three days. She never got sick, though. She could eat, but didn't enjoy it as much as she would have liked. Walking was a bit of a challenge as you might aim for one spot and end up somewhere else. "Pardon me," echoed through the corridors a lot as the passengers passed.

It got too windy to spend much time on deck on this evening. Our dinner was the late one at 8:15 PM. We dined in the Orchid Dining Room. Our waiters, who we would have for the duration of the voyage, were Chris and Aaron. Our dinner companions were Carol and John from Arizona. We ate dinner, walked the deck for a little while and went to bed.

## Episode III – Hilo

By Monday morning, we had established our pattern which we would follow for the rest of the cruise. Up around 6:00 am and pore over maps, planning the day. Then breakfast on deck listening while Hawaiian storyteller Kumu Kahea recites Hawaiian lore. It was standard to cruise at night, port in the morning, sightsee all day and depart at around 5:00 or 6:00 PM for the next port. This Monday morning we breakfasted as Hilo came into view.

Hilo is the main port for the Big Island, also called Hawaii. While the port itself is not much to see, Hilo is pretty. It is on the northeast coast, and because of this, it receives a lot of rain. On all the islands, the north coast is wet, the south coast dry. The mountainous interior of the islands block the rain clouds passage until they have given up most of their moisture. Passing on to the south side, they have no rain to give, creating almost desert-like conditions on the other side of the islands.

Hilo receives almost 400 inches of rain a year, raining almost every day. Streams and waterfalls are plentiful, foliage lush. Hawaii, the Big Island, is the youngest island in the island chain at about a million years old and still growing.

From Hilo, three massive volcanoes are visible in the distance. Mount Kilauea is to the south, Mauna Kea is to the west, and massive Mauna Loa is in the center. Kilauea is the most active of the group, and this was our first destination today. We rented a car from the Alamo Car Rental company. This was the rental company the cruise line provided information for, and since it was the easiest to use, we used it.

We docked by 8:00, had our car by 8:30, and were on the road shortly thereafter. Driving in Hawaii is easy as most highways simply circle the island. The terrain on the interior usually doesn't permit roads across the island. On the first part of the drive to Kilauea, the terrain didn't look much different from Indiana. There are trees on both sides of the road that block the view. There are fields, towns, and other development. Then the trees open up as you go around a bend in the road, and wow - over there is one heck of a mountain.

The road climbs from Hilo to Kilauea, a distance of about 30 miles. We arrived on the volcano about 10:00 AM. We spent some time in the visitor center. This is a National Park, so the facilities are excellent. Here the landscape changes dramatically as you enter Crater Rim Drive. This road circles the crater of Mount Kilauea. The land has become barren rock. The predominate colors are gray, black and grayish-white. Sulfurous steam arises from fissures in the rock. Occasional misty rain falls from dark clouds overhead. Stunted, bent trees cling to the rock. The crater is about 2.5 miles wide, and looks bigger. It looks about thirty miles deep, but in reality is 400 feet. The summit is 4,078 feet above sea level. Nearby Mauna Loa, visible but inaccessible to all but four wheel drive vehicles stands 13, 677 feet above the oceans waves. Those who have read J. R. R. Tolkien's

*Lord of the Rings* will find parallels with Mordor here. Only Mordor is dark and forbidding. This, although barren and desolate, has a beauty that one is difficult to communicate. You have to see it to appreciate it.

Jagger Museum is on the west side of the crater. If one had the time, one could spend hours here looking at the exhibits and reading about volcanoes. Time for us was short, though, so we moved on after fifteen to twenty minutes. The government maintains a Volcano Observatory next to the Museum that does not allow visitors. There are numerous trails branching off Crater Rim Drive. These, if we had time, would provide some interesting hikes. Time didn't permit us to do more than a short jaunt along the crater near the museum. We poked around the volcano about two hours, and then left to return to Hilo to see waterfalls.

Since we didn't want to take the time to return to the ship for lunch, we dined at - MCDONALDS!!!!!!! It was quick, and we didn't want to spend a lot of time eating, as there was much more to see.

Hilo isn't a tourist haven. There are hotels, but not a lot of 'touristy' stuff. It is a pretty town. Tsunamis destroyed the waterfront in1946 and 1960. They have redeveloped it almost exclusively in parks and beaches.

Our first destination was the Wailuku River, on the west side of Hilo and home to several waterfalls. We had time for two, the first being Rainbow Falls. From there we made our way the short distance to Boiling Pots. The name comes from the depressions in the riverbed that make the raging river appear to boil as it passes through the 'pots'. There is a beautiful waterfall here, above the pots.

Now it was time to return to the boat, with time to stop a Queen Liliuokalani Park, along the oceanfront. This is a large Japanese garden, supposed to be the largest of its type outside Japan. Wonderfully maintained, the park is lovely. From an old pier, the SS Independence was visible across the bay.

We returned the car to the nearby airport and took the shuttle back to the ship. The boat departed precisely at 6:00 PM, bound for Hawaii's Kona coast, tomorrow's adventure.

It was again too windy to spend much time on deck after dark. We dined with our dinner companions. At 10:00 the captain had promised a view of the glowing lava fields of Kileae. The passengers gathered on deck to see this spectacle. It was neat, the lava glowing orange/red in the black night. After a short walk around the ship, we retired. Tomorrow would take care of itself.

## Episode IV – Kona Coast

On Tuesday morning, the ship stood off the Kona Coast of The Big Island, on the opposite side of the island from Hilo. The city of Kaliua-Kona has no port, so the passengers go ashore by ferryboat. The *SS Independence* anchored about a mile offshore. This was an interesting operation, loading passengers from one boat to another on the open sea.

What happens is this - the ferryboat stops about 20 feet away from the big ship and crewmen lower a walkway into place between the two ships. Picture this in your mind. The sea is alive - it moves constantly. So does any ship upon its waves. The two boats are in constant motion, up and down, up and down. The walkway is about eight feet wide and moving also, in concert with the boats. I questioned a nearby crewman about the safety of this apparatus. He looked at me and replied that "we usually only loose one or two passengers a trip with this set-up. This is good for the hotels, as the sharks get fed out here, and leave the beaches alone."

His answer did not comfort me much. But ashore we must go, so brave the contraption we did, without incident. Actually, it is quite safe. Crew members line both sides helping passengers who need it. The ride to shore took about ten minutes or so. The ferry held about two hundred people and it was full. From what I saw on this trip, the sharks went hungry.

We pulled up at the dock and disembarked. We would be renting a car again today, so the first order of business was to find the car rental. The rental agency told me that an agent would be waiting for us in a tent by the dock. As we searched for the rental representative, we passed a rather attractive young woman doing the hula. This is a spectacle that you see all over the islands, but this was my first chance to see it up close. What I saw appalled me, but I studied it closely so I could remember how abominable it really was.

Lynne pulled my arm. "Let's go, Casanova, the car rental representative is over here."

I was glad to leave. The Alamo lady led us into a nearby hotel where we filled out the paperwork. She then gave us instructions on how to get out of the city. Our goal for today was to drive through the Kohala Mountains on the north coast of the island and return along the western coast. The Mamalahoa Highway, Route 190, took an inland route to Waimea. This side of the island is in stark contrast to Hilo. Kaliua-Kona receives about five inches of rain a year. This creates desert-like conditions in this side of the island.

The road was good, and followed the mountains, gaining elevation as we approached Waimea. Vegetation here is was sparse. It consists mainly of a grass that rather resembles foxtail. Except that, it is much fuller than foxtail and an emerald green with silvery seedpods that shimmer in the golden sunlight. This grass contrasted with the black volcanic rock in which it grew. Gnarled trees dotted the landscape, highlighted by rather large prickly pear cactus. The terrain was mountainous to the north and east. To the south we could see occasional glimpses of the sapphire blue

Pacific. This was one of the most beautiful drives I have taken in my life. The landscape is so unusual and unexpected for Hawaii; one is awestruck by its stark beauty.

We reached Waimea and proceeded northwest on the Kohala Mountains Road to Hawi, on the extreme north coast. This road is narrower, and windier than our previous route, but no less lovely. Trees were more numerous here, as was the vegetation.

Hawi marked the farthest north we could go without a boat. We turned south, with reluctance, on the 'Akoni Pule Highway, bound for Kawaihae. We stopped at Mahukona Beach Park to admire the ocean. We were lucky enough to get there just in time to see whales cavorting just offshore, maybe 200 yards or so. We watched them for a while, until they swam out to sea. By this time, it was about dinnertime, and we were looking for something to eat. As it was sparse pickings out here, we ALMOST ate at a truck stop. However, I saw it too late to turn, and being too lazy to turn around and go back, I drove on. We continued down the coast to Hapuna Beach State Recreation Area. As we pulled in, Lynne noticed that they had a hamburger stand. We pulled in and had some of the best hamburgers you could ask for, a wonderful view of the beach, AND LOTS OF BABES.

Upon finishing our meal, we spent some time walking the beach. I wouldn't go in the water because I knew that the sharks hadn't fed that morning. It was a nice beach, and the water that splashed our feet was cool and nice.

As we had arranged for late tours in Kona, we had to leave, continuing down the coast. We picked up the Queen Kaahumanu Highway, Route 19, at Kawaihae. There is a lot of development along this stretch of highway. This is the preferred destination for beach-dwelling tourists, because it seldom rains here.

Returning to Kaliua-Kona, we returned our car and headed to the dock. We boarded a glass-bottomed boat for a lazy man's view of the fishes and sea bottom. I say lazy man's method, because you can take snorkel expeditions. My theory is that there are some things you don't do for the first time after you pass forty. These include skiing, skydiving, and snorkeling. So we made our way for the boat. It was an interesting ride, lasting about forty-five minutes. We saw many fish, the reef, and had an entertaining guide.

Our next stop was just a short distance away, a horse carriage ride through Kona. If you ever get the opportunity to do this - don't. It is expensive, you really don't get to see much, and in our case, the horse was much more entertaining than the driver was. He expected a tip. We gave one, painfully.

Upon completing this, we returned to the ship on the last ferry. The ship departed at 6:00 PM., after which we showered and dressed for dinner. This was the first night that you could stand being on deck for any length of time, as the wind had died down. We explored the ship and retired for the night.

## Episode V

## Oahu - Honolulu

Our destination upon leaving the Kona Coast was the island of Oahu, specifically the Port of Honolulu. The approach to Honolulu from the sea was not as impressive as our earlier air approach had been, but we could see more. The SS Independence docked on a pier next to downtown Honolulu. We exited the ship right into a downtown shopping mall. This mall is similar to Circle Center Mall for those of you familiar with the development in downtown Indianapolis. It's pretty cool to step out of a ship and walk down the gangplank into the second story of a major downtown shopping mall.

Our plans for the day were to rent a car and circle the eastern portion of the island. Oahu is small enough you could circle the entire island in a day if you didn't want to stop to see anything. Our car rental company picked us up right outside the door of the mall in a shuttle bus and took us to their office. Here we filled out the paperwork for the car, and were off once again.

If you want an interesting experience, take a country boy; drop him down in the middle of a major city with which he is unfamiliar. Then give him a map that doesn't tell him everything he needs to know. Further, put him further east on the map than he thinks he is. Then stick in three major highways going the same direction. One of these is directly over one of the others, the lower one not really shown on the map. Throw in a boatload of traffic just to stir the pot a little. You start out on the lower highway, needing to be on the upper one. This he tries like hell to get to do, and after he gets there, he's not sure he is even going the right direction. Throw in a copilot who can't read maps and questions every move he makes. Now you have all the ingredients for the suspenseful beginning of a journey.

The incident actually turned out well. The pilot followed his instincts. He was going the right direction. And after twenty-five years with the same co-pilot, has learned not to argue with the cockpit crew. Just shut-up and drive! Honolulu is a pretty big town, about 700,000, laid out long and narrow. They have no choice, with the ocean in front and a mountain range behind. It does make for an interesting road system.

Our route for the day would take us north on the Kamehameha Highway, Route 99, towards the north shore of Oahu. The highway would take us between two mountain ranges, the Koolau range on the east and the Waianae Range on the west. We would also pass the Wheeler Army Airfield and Schofield Barracks. This was the route over which the Japanese attack on Pearl Harbor came, we learned the next day. The Japanese carriers sat well to the north. The attacking planes flew low down this valley between two mountain ranges and attacked the base. Then they turned around over the ocean and gave them hell again as they returned to their waiting ships. It was a good plan, with devastating consequences for both countries, as it turned out.

We continued north until we reached the town of Haleiwa, on the north shore. Here we caught Route 83 east for the drive along the coast. This highway follows the coast for most of the north and east shore of the island. This is a pretty drive with lots of beaches to pull into to walk, surf, or swim. We stopped right away, at Haleiwa Beach Park. We walked a bit, watched what few surfers there were, and took to the road again.

Our next stop was the Waimea Valley Adventure Park. Here we merely drove in the parking lot, looked around, and drove out. Admittance to the park was $25 each and since we didn't plan to spend much time there, we drove on.

We lunched on Subway sandwiches at the Laie-Maloo Beach Park, near Laie. By the way, if you ever get the opportunity to go to Hawaii, when you get hungry and see a restaurant, go there. You may not get another chance to eat, as there don't seem to be many places to eat away from the big cities.

We sat on a log on this beach eating and watching the waves. There weren't many people here now. I noticed a small island just off the shore. There was a large kite near this island, and I assumed that some one on the island was flying it. My copilot noticed that the kite was moving around a lot. I wondered what kind of drugs were in the sandwich she was eating. But watching the kite, I realized she was right. It was moving and the kite was being pulled along over the waves of the ocean by a person riding a small surfboard. Our server in the ship's restaurant, Chris, told me that night that the board was called a boogie board. This is a sawed off little brother of the surfboard. And of course, the fellow we were watching was wind surfing.

I had noticed something that was dispelling a myth that maybe you have. I was under the assumption that Hawaii was a big tourist haven, but this is simply not true. As we drove around, I noticed that all the cars have Hawaiian licensee plates. Even in lowly Indiana, you see plates from other states, but not in Hawaii! This proves that no one goes there. Maybe if they built a road here, they would get some tourists.

From the beach, we drove on south and visited the Polynesian Cultural Center just south of Laie. This attraction was built and maintained by the Mormon Church. It has various Polynesian village exhibits laid out. There are interpreters from the particular island depicted staffing the exhibit. The interpreters are college students from nearby Brigham Young University. They work off part of their college tuition by working in the Center. Tahiti, Samoa, Hawaii, Fiji, the Marquesas, New Zealand, and Tonga native cultures are represented here. BYU recruits students from these islands to come to the University. You can take a tram tour of the BYU campus and nearby Mormon Temple. We didn't do this, as time didn't permit it, but we did enjoy the visit to the Center. It is a bit 'touristy', but worth the time and admission cost - $27 each.

We continued on our journey along the coast, stopping at Kuala Point to walk the beach and watch the ocean. Lots of birds, including cardinals. How the state bird of Indiana got here, with no road to drive on is beyond me, but there they were. Who would have believed it?

Upon leaving Kualoa Point, I ACTUALLY MADE A MISTAKE! The plan was to drive on to the Pali Highway at Kailua and over look Honolulu from the Pali Lookout. Then drive on back to Honolulu through the Pali Tunnel. But I misread the signs, and I turned too soon. By the time I realized my mistake, the traffic was getting heavy, and we were getting tired. Moreover, time was too short to turn around and go back. We had to get the car back to the car rental by 7:00 PM to catch the shuttle back to the boat. The next, and last, shuttle from the car rental to the boat was at 9:00, too late for us to get our dinner. And I wanted my dinner!

So we ended up back at the car rental at 5:30 instead of 6:30 like I'd planned. We cooled our heels at the rental company office for an hour, awaiting our bus.

We arrived back at the ship in time to clean up and dress for dinner. Our normal dinner companions had gone to a luau.

Therefore, the server sat us at a different table with a couple from Michigan named Jack and Peggy. Their last name unfortunately I can't remember. The other couple ordered escargot, and offered us a taste. After a bit of trepidation, we did try one. It actually tastes good, for a snail. It's kind of like mushrooms in flavor.

After dining, we left the ship to wander in the shopping center. All the shops were closed, but the nightspots were all open. As if we spend a lot of time in night spots! It was fun walking, though. After thoroughly tiring ourselves out, we retired for the night.

This is where Lynne finally got rid of her slight 'sea queasies'. The ship was in port all night, so we didn't do any rocking' and rolling'. She enjoyed her dinner, and the 'queasies' didn't come back the next day when we got under way again.

## Episode VI - Honolulu

At breakfast this morning, we are still in Honolulu Harbor watching the activity in the harbor. It is a busy port. One topic of conversation is the plight of the SS Patriot, another cruise liner owned by American Cruise Lines.

The SS Patriot, the SS Independence's sister ship, sits next door to us in the harbor. The passengers on this ship have had a bit of bad luck that has turned into good luck, I think. Recently refurbished, the SS Patriot was to begin its maiden voyage. It is a European ship, and the American Cruise Line personnel are not familiar with the engineering on the ship. It developed engine trouble soon after putting out to sea, and had to dock here in Honolulu. It has been here since Sunday, not moving. The passengers have not gotten to see any of the other islands. Rumor has it that they have received a full refund and will get one-half off another cruise. Meanwhile, they can stay on the ship and visit Honolulu. Or go home if they wish. I looked into booking that boat originally. But I couldn't find enough information on the internet. Being too lazy to use the phone, I booked the SS Independence instead. I'm not sure if I'm glad or sad.

At any rate, today we are off to see Pearl Harbor, for which we booked a tour through the Cruise Line. There are many good tours available like this, many going to the places we have gone. We just like to tour on our own, so most of the time we have rented a car. The bus leaves for Pearl Harbor at 8:00 AM from the bus kiosk across the street from the mall. We board the bus, and we are off.

As we rode the bus over to the Harbor, it strikes me how small the world has gotten by the composition of the bus passengers. The couple in front of me is speaking English in a heavy German accent. Across the aisle near the front, a lady speaks with a New England accent. Behind her, we hear a rich South Carolina drawl. Lynne and I are from the Midwest and another couple behind have a northern timbre to their voice. Scattered throughout the bus are numerous nationalities - Japanese, Chinese, and God knows what else. All corners of America and the world come together in one little bus here in Honolulu.

Our driver pulls into the lot at Pearl Harbor and keeps us together so we all get tickets for the same movie and tour boat. The tour consists of a twenty-minute movie about the attack, museum visit, and a boat ride out to the Arizona Memorial. We line up, get our tickets, and wait for his instructions. We have over an hour to wait until our movie starts, so he tells us to enjoy the museum and park grounds. We wander through the museum, looking at the various exhibits, scale boat and plane models, and displays. A veteran of the attack speaks of his experiences on December 7, 1941.

Now the movie, which is an excellent production abut the attack and the events surrounding it. After the movie, we board the boat that takes us out to the Arizona. A Memorial floats over the stricken ship, which is still visible under the water. And yes, oil does still bubble out from the ship. The battleship US Missouri sits near where the Arizona lays. It is fitting to see the warship that symbolizes the beginning of the war near the ship the Japanese Empire surrendered on, ending it. It is sobering to see old men, obviously war veterans, still moved by the emotion of this place. The visitors, young and old are silent as we board our boat for the return to shore. We return to the bus, and leave the ghosts of war behind.

On our return, the driver informs us we have the option of going to Hilo Hatties. This is a large department store featuring all things Hawaiian. We opt to go and see this store that we have heard so much about. The bus driver drops us off out front, and we enter. It is definitely an unusual store. The clothing is all made in Hawaii. To prove it you can look through large glass windows at the sewing room in which it seamstresses sit, sewing. It is a small sewing factory, about the size of a decent-sized basketball gym. There are probably fifty to seventy five women working at sewing machines making clothes.

Hilo Hatties is a big store, boasting outlets all over Hawaii. They stock just about anything you can imagine, and many things you can't imagine. We spend about an hour or more padding about the place, picking up a few souvenirs and just being tourists.

The store runs a free shuttle that will take us back to the boat. We lunch on the boat, and wander around the Mall and downtown Honolulu, seeing the sights. The boat will leave promptly at 5:00, so we don't have time to stray too far. We ride the elevator to the top of the nearby Aloha Tower for a panoramic view of the city and the harbor.

The going away ceremony at the pier features singing, a hula, and various other going's on. A fireboat parades behind us through the harbor, spraying fountains of water, which I regard as a terrible waste of water. It is impressive, though.

The boat pulls away from the pier, and we have departed. The city of Honolulu, and the island of Oahu slowly slip away. As we leave the harbor, we are lucky enough see a pod of dolphins shooting gracefully through the waves in escort. All this, and the sunset over the water was gorgeous that evening.

After dining, we walked out on deck to enjoy the pleasant evening. We noticed a rather large city along the shore of an island near the ship. I couldn't figure out where we were. Lynne said it looked like Honolulu. But since we had left Honolulu five hours earlier, it couldn't be. Then, against the background of stars and lights on the island, it appeared the ship was moving backward. This was disconcerting to say the least. With the pitching and rolling of the ocean, to feel like we were moving backwards was a little too much to take, so we went quickly below deck. We found out later that the seas further out were rough. So the captain elected to go in circles just offshore from Honolulu as he waited for most passengers to bed down for the night before going to sea.

That was enough of that. Aloha!

## Episode Vii – Kauai Friday

Our journey through the Hawaiian Islands next took us to the Garden Isle, Kauai. This is the oldest island in the chain, around six million years old. It is also the western-most and the fourth largest of the eight main islands. A single volcano forms the island. The remains of the volcano, called Mt. Waialeale, are the wettest spot on earth, receiving over 500 inches of rain a year.

Besides all this, it is the most beautiful island to approach from the sea. We advanced from the east, the sunrise behind us illuminating the mountains on the southern side of the islands. Whale sightings and a fantastic double rainbow that framed the harbor greeted our arrival.

After docking, we got our car and drove off into those southern mountains that had looked so beautiful from the sea. Our route was towards the Waimea Canyon, also called the Grand Canyon of the Pacific. We were about to find out why it was so named. The road was narrow and winding, with numerous look outs for viewing the magnificent scenery. A hurricane in 1991 flattened Kauai. The storm flattened everything. Trees, buildings, homes - all were gone. In the ten years since this tragedy, the forests have largely regenerated, although the trees are all small, yet.

They rebuilt the homes and businesses with massive aid from the other islands. Authorities relocated most of the population elsewhere. Remarkably, only one or two people died.

I'm still trying to decide which is the most magnificent drive we took. It is either the trip along the Kona Coast on Hawaii, or this journey along the crest of the Waimea Canyon Drive. The route goes up to Kokee State Park and the Kalalau lookout. It might be a draw. We stopped at most of the canyon overlooks, each higher and more spectacular than the one before. By the time we finally got up to the main canyon lookout, the clouds had moved in, blocking the view. This lookout is at an elevation of 4000 feet, so it is high enough to get in the clouds.

We drove on to the Kalalau Lookout, about four miles beyond, which is a dramatic view of the Pacific. Clouds still were hanging around here, so we didn't get to see anything. At this point, we had to turn around and go back down the way we had come, as the road ended at a cliff 4077 feet above the ocean. By the time we returned to the main canyon overlook, it had rained, clearing the sky.

The Waimea River has spent millions of years carving out this canyon, and I think it was time well spent. It is easily one of the most spectacular sights one could ever hope to see. Helicopters bringing passengers to an aerial view of the canyon looked like tiny toys in the distance. A distant waterfall plunged into the river from the heights of a far away valley. Some goats were just discernible far down on a ridge. This was another of many scenes we had to tear ourselves away from reluctantly.

We wound our way back down the highway, seeing the landscape in an entirely different light. We returned to the main highway, Kaumualii Highway, Route 50. On our way back through Kalaheo, we again dined at McDonald's. Our next destination was Wailua Falls, which was the waterfall featured on the show 'Fantasy Island'. The falls are nice, but the angle from which you get to see them is not too good. But what was that sound? Somewhere in the distance, I heard the plaintive cry, "De plane, De plane, Boss, de plane".

Our afternoon tour included Opaekaa Falls and a short visit to the banks of the Wailua River, the only navigable river in Hawaii. There is a riverboat that plies the waters of this lovely river on its way to Fern Grotto. We didn't do this, but we did see the boat.

From here, we drove north of Highway 56 until we got to Kapaa Beach Park. This was as far north as we would go, for it was time to return to the ship. We walked along this beach, watching swimmers brave the surf. At another beach just south of here, we stopped and managed to glimpse two whales just offshore. Oh, for a fishing pole.

We ran into heavy traffic on the highway home, and just barely got back to the car rental in time to catch the last shuttle to the boat. We didn't have to worry about them leaving us, though, because the first mate of the ship was also in this group.

Once back on the boat, we spent some time doing some packing, as this was our last full day on the boat. Spotted two whales close to the boat. We dined and did more packing. We have to be out of our room by 8:30 AM tomorrow

## Episode VII– Maui And Home

This was our last day in Hawaii. Our ship returned to the place we started, Maui, at 8:00 AM. We had to be out of the cabin by 8:30. Up at 5:00 to finish packing, we breakfasted at dawn on deck to the same spectacular view we had seen the first morning. Was that just a week ago? It seemed much longer. We had a good cruise. The weather was almost perfect, most experiences good. The cruise personnel told us that the week before this had been terrible. Rain and floods on Kona, of all places. Heavy seas and rain most other places.

Since our plane didn't leave Kahului Airport until 2:00 PM, we had time to do a little sightseeing before we left. The cruise line would take our luggage over to the airport, so we didn't need to pack anything along. We had signed up for a tour of the Maui Ocean Center, which is on the south shore of Maui. Since it is through the narrow part of the island, it is only about a half hour away.

The bus picked us up at the dock. The Maui Ocean Center is an oceanfront aquarium. We had about two hours to spend, and that is just about the right amount of time to plan for if you are ever in the area. It has many large aquarium exhibits featuring local salt-water fish. There are also smaller exhibits featuring just a few organisms. A tip to the traveler. Aquarium personnel get a little testy if they catch you looking at the fish with a jar of tartar sauce and rye bun in your hand!

The best part of the Ocean Center is the under-sea tunnel. It doesn't really go under the ocean, but one feels like one is beneath the waves among the fishes. The tunnel is about 75 feet long, 8 feet high and wide enough for two benches and an aisle between. Manta Rays, sharks, and other assorted fish swim all around. The other exhibits in the Ocean Center are excellent, but this is extraordinary!

We boarded the bus at around 11:30 AM. The bus dropped us off at the airport by 11:45. We claimed our luggage from the cruise lines, checked it in at the airport desk for the flight home, and were ready to leave. Our final meal in Hawaii consisted of hot dogs, potato chips, and fruit juice. We boarded the plane at 2:00 PM, bound for Los Angeles, Flight 42, Gate 29.

The flight was uneventful, landing at LA around 6:35, Hawaii Time. At LA, we had a long layover - our flight didn't leave until 10:55. All times for the flights home will be in Hawaii Time to make it easier to figure flight time. There is a five-hour difference between Indiana and Hawaii.

At Los Angeles Airport, we ran into a couple from Indianapolis - June and Charles Wood. They helped make the layover a little shorter than it would have been otherwise. Our flight left LA about 10:55 PM, arriving at Chicago around 2:45 am. I don't remember much about this flight, as I went to sleep shortly after take-off.

We didn't have much time in Chicago, the flight to Cincinnati departing at 3:10 AM. We almost ran through the airport to get to the plane. We made the connection, our luggage did not. Arrival in Cincinnati was at 3:55 AM. We dined at a Steak and Shake in Lawrenceburg and were home around 6:15 AM. This was 11:15 Indiana time. It was about 40 degrees and sunny. That was not a bad day for Indiana, but hard to take after 80 degrees.

## Types of Hawaiian Cruises

Four different types of cruises await the traveler to Hawaii. These are:

Exclusive Hawaiian Cruise

Point-to-Point-Hawaiian Cruise

Combination Hawaiian Cruise

Small Ship Hawaiian Cruise

Exclusive Hawaiian Cruise

These Hawaiian Cruises begin and end in the Hawaiian Islands. Typically, they are seven days, but other lengths are available.

Point to Point-Hawaiian Cruises

These cruises begin in a port on either Hawaii or on the mainland. They end at another point. These usually last around fifteen days.

Combination Cruises

These cruises combine Hawaii with the Polynesian Islands. These cruises can last from fifteen days and up.

Small Ship Hawaiian Cruises

These cruises are on smaller ships than the typical Hawaiian Cruise. They are able to visit ports and islands that the bigger boats cannot get into.

Celebrity Cruises

Sailing from Ensenada, Mexico to Hilo, Honolulu, Kailua Kona, Lahaina, Nawiliwili and Vancouver, Canada.

Norwegian Cruise Line

NCL's Pride of America makes weekly voyages from Honolulu. It has port stops at Hilo on the Big Island,

Kahului on Maui, Kona on the Big Island and Lihue on Kauai.

Princess Cruises

Offering several cruises to Hawaii from Ensenada, Mexico; Los Angeles; Tahiti and Vancouver, Canada.

Royal Caribbean Cruises

## Hawaii Small Ship Cruises

Many of these cruises are on yachts that hold less than a hundred people, some much less. These smaller ships can visit little known coves and inlets that the larger cruise ships cannot go. Most offer excursions to kayak, snorkel and interact with wildlife on an intimate level. The Hawaiian Island chain consists of over a hundred islands. The big ships focus on the four largest islands, Hawaii, Maui, Kwauel, and Oahu. Smaller ships sometimes will visit smaller, unanimated or sparsely inhabitant isles.

Small ship cruises usually are a weeklong. There are itineraries that are shorter and longer depending upon the needs of the traveler. Many of these cruises are "unstructured." They are spontaneous cruises that take advantage of weather conditions and wildlife activity. They then set their destinations accordingly. Visitors may explore the islands by foot, kayak, paddleboard, sailboat, mountain bike or motor launch. Many of the cruises allow passengers to meet local Hawaiian's at their homes and on their land. This provides a more intimate exposure to Hawaiian culture.

American Safari Cruise

USA River Cruises

Sunstone Tours & Cruises

Star of Honolulu

Wild Side Specialty Tours

Small Ships of Princess

Tauck

Adventuresmith Explorations

Smithsonian Journeys

## Exclusive Hawaiian Cruise - Big Ship

These big ship cruises typically visit four of the seven inhabited Hawaiian Islands, Maui, Oahu, Hawaii, usually called the Big Island, and Kuwaii. Usually seven or eight days in length the cruise offers the full amenities of the big cruise ship and many shore excursions for the passenger to experience many activities on the islands and the waters surrounding them. These cruises begin at a Hawaiian port and end at the same port.

By United States Law, only American flagged ships may cruise all American ports.

<u>Norwegian</u>

## Point to Point Hawaiian Cruises

**Big Ship**

These cruises are usually longer in duration than the Exclusive Hawaiian Cruises. The usual time length is eleven to fifteen days. The traveler will spend much more time at sea during one of these cruises. Usually the time at sea is four to five days.

Typical ports on the mainland for the cruise to originate or end are:

Vancouver

British Columbia

Los Angeles

California

San Diego

Long Beach

San Pedro

Ensenada, Mexico.

**Typical Hawaiin ports of call are:**

Hilo (Big Island)

Maui (Kahului)

Honolulu

Kauai (Nawiliwili)

Nawiliwili (Kauai)

Lahaina (Maui)

Kona (Big Island).

Honolulu is the most popular Hawaiian origination point for cruises beginning in Hawaii. Some of the major lines that offer these cruises include:

Royal Caribbean International

Princess Cruises

Carnival Cruise Lines.

Holland America Line

Celebrity Cruises

## Combination Cruises

### Big Ship

These cruises combine Hawaii with the Polynesian Islands. These cruises can last from fifteen days and up. Popular Combination Cruises combine Hawaiian cruises with cruises to Tahiti, Marquesas, French Polynesia are one way, longer than a week, and often include Papeete, Bora Bora, and Moorea.

In some cases you'll n  and other South Pacific Islands. These cruises can be very long, up to thirty five days and more.

Crystal Cruises.

Holland America Line

Princess Cruises

### Norwegian Hawaiian Cruse

Norwegian Cruise Line

1-866-234-7350

http://www.ncl.com

The Norwegian Cruise Line began life in 1966 as the Norwegian Caribbean Line. It's headquarters is in Miami-Dade County.  Star Cruises owns the line. Norwegian Cruise Lines currently operates twelve ships. These are the ships currently used for the Hawaiian Cruise vacations.

### Pride of America

Norwegian ships offer numerous dining options.

On the *Pride of America* you will find these restaurants:

Jefferson's Bistro

Lazy J Texas Steakhouse

Liberty Main Dining Room

Little Italy

24-hour Room Service

Skyline Main Dining Room

Sushi Bar

Teppanyaki

Aloha Café

Cadillac Diner

John Adam's Coffee Bar

24-hour Pizza Delivery

Key West Bar & Grill

Norwegian Cruise Line features a cruise concept called Freestyle Cruising®. Most cruise lines assign a dining room and dining partners for your evening meal. Formal, or at least dress, attire is required in the dining room. Norwegian allows you to choose where you want to eat from amongst almost twenty dining rooms and there is no dress code. There are no fixed dining times or places on a Norwegian Cruise.

Ports and Places a Norwegian Hawaii Cruise Might Visit:

Hilo

Honolulu

Kahului

Kona

Kauai

Norwegian Cruise Lines offers a multitude of shore excursions. These range from submarine tours to beach walks. You may reserve shore excursions for up to two days before your sailing date. It is best to reserve your shore excursions ahead. This is because there are a limited number of people which may partake in most shore excursions and they tend to fill up quickly. When you enroll in a shore excursion Norwegian Cruise Line makes all the arrangements. This includes pick up and delivery at the pier. You do not have to pay in advance for shore excursions. The line bills your room account for them. For more information, please visit the Norwegian Cruise Line Web site.

Onboard entertainment on the Pride of America includes:

Outdoor Chess

Golf Driving Net & Putting Green

Gyrosphere

Hollywood Theatre

Hot Tubs (6)

Internet Centre

Jogging/Walking Track

LifeStyles Room

Meeting Rooms & Auditorium Area

Newbury Street Shops

Oasis Pool

The Conservatory

Photo Gallery

The Chapel

Rascals Kid's Club

Santa Fe Fitness Centre

Library

Santa Fe Spa

South Beach Pool

Shuffles Card Room

SoHo Art Gallery

Basketball/Volleyball/Tennis Court

Blast Off Video Arcade

You will find four basic stateroom types - Inside  Oceanview  Balcony  Suite. All of these are available in different sizes to accommodate differing numbers of guests from two to six. All staterooms have a phone, TV, air conditioning, refrigerator, safe, duvet, bathroom with shower and a hair dryer. Most lower beds are convertible to a queen-size bed.

**Royal Caribbean International**

Inside US (866) 562-7625

Outside US+1 (305) 341-0204

http://www.royalcaribbean.com/

Royal Caribbean International is owned by Royal Caribbean Cruises Ltd. and is an American and Norwegian owned cruise line based in Miami, Florida. There are currently twenty-two ships in service, each ship's name ending in "of the Seas."

Royal Caribbean International offers ten, eleven, twelve and thirteen night cruises. These point-to-point cruises begin in either Vancouver, British Columbia or Honolulu and end in either Vancouver or Honolulu.

Typical Ports of Call of a Royal Caribbean International Hawaiian Cruise

Honolulu (Oahu),

Ala Moana Boulevard

Diamond Head

Koko Head

Polynesian Cultural Center

Oahu's North Shore

Paradise Cove Luau

Nawiliwili (Kauai)

Uluwehi Falls

Waimea Canyon,

Lumahai Beach

Bali Ha'i Mountains

Lahaina (Maui),

Haleakala Crater

Iao Valley State Park

Maui Tropical Plantation.

Mount Kilauea

Kailua Kona

Kohala

Pololu Valley

Kapoloa Falls

Hilo

Hawaii Volcanoes National Park

Lava Tree State Park

Hawaii Tropical Botanical Garden

Victoria, British Columbia

Vancouver, British Columbia

**Things to Do On Board a Royal Caribbean Ship**

FlowRider® - 40-foot-long surf simulator

Rock climbing - Forty foot tall rock climbing wall

Zip line over nine decks

Ice skating rink

Fitness center

Fitness classes

Mini golf

Sports court and tournaments

Boxing ring

Jogging track

Inline skating

Table tennis

Scuba in the pool

A Viking Crown Lounge resides at the top of each ship of the Royal Caribbean International line. This lounge affords a breathtaking view of the ocean as you drink, dance or just relax. Many decks have atriums and there is an extensive selection of onboard entertainment. The ships of Royal Caribbean International are huge, in excess of 2500 passengers, and afford many amenities for your Alaskan cruise.

## Carnival Cruise Lines

Carnival Cruises

1.800.764.7419

http://www.carnival.com/

Carnival Cruise Line is a British owned cruise line based in Dorel, Florida, which is a suburb of Miami, Florida. The cruise line's ships have a reputation as the "Fun Ships." This reputation is because of the casino like atmosphere on the ships and the variety of fun filled ship activities. Carnival's 23 ships account for almost twenty percent of worldwide cruise ship revenue. Carnival has become famous for its shorter, less expensive cruises.

## Typical Hawaiian Ports of Call:

Hilo, HI

Maui (Kahului), HI

Honolulu, HI

Kauai (Nawiliwili), HI

Kona, HI

## Typical Carnival Cruise amenities are:

Some of the most spacious staterooms at sea

Delicious dining - including 24 hour room service

A variety of onboard entertainment

Fun-filled youth programs

Award winning stage shows

The most beautiful destinations

Carnival Cruise offers a wide variety of shore excursions for which the passenger will pay a separate charge. You may select from a variety of staterooms.

**Interior Rooms**

These rooms offer excellent values and these spacious accommodations include generous amenities.

Ocean View Rooms - The large stateroom windows give you excellent views of the ocean and each destination.

Balcony Rooms - With a balcony room you may sit outdoors, relax, enjoy the privacy and admire the passing scenery.

Suite - these extra-large accommodations have a separate sitting area and spacious balcony.

**Grand Suite**

The Grand Suites have the same features as a Suite plus a walk-in closet and whirlpool bath.

**Excursions:**

Excursions can include:

Snorkeling

Sailing

Glass bottomed boats

Rafting

Helicopter tours

Submarine tours

Holland America Line

1-877-932-4259

http://www.hollandamerica.com/

A Dutch passenger and shipping company founded in 1873, the Netherlands-America Steamship Company has transformed into Holland America Line. The Holland America Line's headquarters is in Seattle, Washington and is a British owned cruise line. The Holland America Line operates fifteen ships. It offers cruises to seven continents. It anticipates serving 750,000 cruise passengers in 2012. The Holland America Line also operates the Westmark Hotel chain in Alaska and the Yukon Territory in Canada.

Holland America Line has mid size ships which carry fewer passengers than some of the other cruise lines. Cruises originate or end at San Diego. Holland America Line offers combination Mexico/Hawaii, and Hawaii/Tahiti/Marquesas cruises. These range in length from fourteen to twenty-eight days. There is one forty two day cruise that includes the Panama Canal.

**Ports of Call or Sightseeing for Most Cruises**

Hilo

Honolulu

Nawiliwili (Kauai)

Lahaina

**Amenities Found on a Holland America Ship:**

Spacious staterooms

Gracious, award-winning service

Wraparound teak decks

Fresh floral arrangements

Explorations Café, powered by The New York Times

Greenhouse Spa & Salon

Two outdoor pools, one with retractable roof

The Retreat, resort-style pool experience

Mirabella, luxury jewelry salon

As You Wish® dining

Complimentary 24/7 in-room dining

Pinnacle Grill

Tamarind, Pan-Asian dining

Canaletto, relaxed Italian fare

Lido Café, relaxed, casual, quick

Main Dining Room, two-tier, sophisticated, flexible

Mix, featuring specialty bars with Champagne, Martinis, and Spirits & Ales

**Activities Found on a Holland America Ship:**

Culinary Arts Center, presented by Food & Wine magazine

Renowned guest chefs

Digital Workshop, powered by Windows®

Self-guided iPod® tours of onboard art collection

Half Moon Cay, award-winning private island

Royal Dutch High Tea

Northern Lights Nightclub

Crow's Nest, lookout by day, dance club by night

Musical productions, concerts and stage shows

Casino

Piano Bar

Show Lounge, Movie Theater & Disco

Sports Bar featuring ESPN International

Club HAL® for kids & tweens

The Loft and The Oasis for teens

Private in-room movie viewing

Pilates, Yoga, Aerobics, Cardio, Ki-Bo, Circuit Training & Aquarobics

Duty-free shopping

Shore Excursion Collections: Medallion, Encore, World Wonders & Signature

**Stateroom Amenities:**

Spacious, elegantly appointed staterooms, many with private verandahs

Luxurious Mariner's Dream™ beds and premium linens

Daily housekeeping to tidy belongings and keep staterooms immaculate

Large, extra-fluffy Egyptian cotton towels

Lighted magnifying mirrors; massage showerheads; salon-quality hair dryers

Luxurious terry cloth bathrobes

Elemis Aromapure "Time to Spa" bath amenities

Televisions with DVD players

Generous storage

Complimentary fresh fruit

Complimentary 24-hour in-room dining

Nightly turndown service

Complimentary shoeshine service

Complimentary ice service

## Princess Hawaiian Cruises

1-800-774-6237

http://www.princess.com/

Princess Cruises is part of a family of ten cruise companies owned by Carnival Cruises. Santa Clarita, California is the cruise lines base. They used two of the company's ships, Island Princess and Pacific Princess, in the television series The Love Boat. Princess Cruises began in 1965 with one ship, the Princess Patricia. The company pioneered wintertime cruises in the tropics. Its second ship, Italia, was the first was the first to open up the upper deck by having its lifeboats mounted lower down on the ship.

### Dining Options on a Princess Cruise:

### Anytime or Traditional Dining

Traditional Dining allows you to dine at set times with the same table mates and wait staff each evening.

Anytime Dining* offers you the freedom to dine with whom you choose, anytime between 5:30 p.m. and 10 PM. You may choose from a selection of elegant, upscale restaurants.

### Specialty Restaurants

Sabatini's

Crown Grill

Sterling Steakhouse

Bayou Cafe & Steakhouse

The Piazza

Horizon Court

Ultimate Balcony Dining

### Hawaiian Destinations

Hilo

Honolulu

Kauai

Maui

**Points of Interest:**

**Hilo**

Hawaii Volcanoes National Park

Tropical Botanical Gardens

Akaka or Rainbow Falls

Waipi'o Valle

Mauna Kea

Kealakekua Bay

Lava Tree State Park

**Oahu**

Pearl Harbor & USS Arizona Memorial

Polynesian Cultural Center

Pali Lookout

Diamond Head Crater

Iolani Palace

Queen Emma Summer Palace

Hanauma Bay

Waimea Bay and North Shore

**Kauai (Nawiliwili)**

Waimea Canyon

Wailua River & Fern Grotto

Na Pali Coast

North Shore of Kauai

Grove Farm Homestead

Kilaueau Lighthouse

**Kona**

Place of Refuge

Kealakelua Bay & Captain Cook Monument

Aquatic Adventures

Volcanoes National Park

Kona Coffee Sampling

Cloud Forest Sanctuary

**Excursions can include:**

Snorkeling

Sailing

Glass bottomed boats

Rafting

Helicoptor tours

Submarine tours

Princess offers a Polynesian Islands cruise that begins in Sydney, Australia. It returns there thirty-five days later. Ports visited on this cruise include:

Nuku'alofa, Tonga

Apia, Western Samoa

Cross International Date Line

Honolulu, Hawaii

Maui (Lahaina), Hawaii

Kauai (Nawiliwili), Hawaii

Kona, Hawaii

Hilo, Hawaii

Tahiti (Papeete), French Polynesia

Moorea, Polynesia

Bora Bora, French Polynesia

Pago Pago, American Samoa

Suva, Fiji

Noumea, New Caledonia

Sydney, Australia

Princess also offers a roundtrip cruise that begins and terminates in Los Angeles, California.


**Celebrity Cruises**

(866) 592-7225

http://www.celebritycruises.com/

Celebrity is one of five cruise lines owned by Royal Caribbean Cruises Ltd. This is the company formed by the merger of Celebrity Cruises Ltd and Royal Caribbean International in 1997. The other cruise lines owned by Royal Caribbean Cruises Ltd. are Royal Caribbean International, Azamara Club Cruises, Pullmantur Cruises and CDF Croisieres de France. The company has its headquarters in Miami, Florida.


The ship currently (2012) operates eleven ships in four classes. Celebrity is famous for its elegant ships, dining and overall cruise experience. Many consider it the marquis line of Royal Caribbean offering a first class cruise experience.

**Ships:**

Celebrity Century

Celebrity Millennium

Celebrity Solstice

**Ports Visited:**

San Diego

California

Honolulu

Oahu

Kailua/Kona

Lahaina, Maui

Hilo

Ensenada, Mexico

San Diego, California

Celebrity Cruises typically begin and end in San Diego, California. These are fourteen-day cruises. Shorter ten or eleven day cruises begin on Ensenada, Mexico or Honolulu and end in Honolulu or Ensenada, Mexico.

**Ports or Attractions That You May Visit During a Celebrity Cruise:**

**Hilo, Hawaii**

Hawaii Tropical Botanical Garden HL09

Rainbow Falls

Boiling Pots

Kaumanu Caves

**Honolulu (Oahu), Hawaii**

Arizona Memorial

Pearl Harbor

Battleship Missouri.

North Shore HN15

Ka'a'awa Valley

Kualoa

Diamond Head

Halona Point

Makapu'u Lookout,

Pali Lookout

Nuuanu Valley,

Waimanalo community

Nuuanu Valley

Punchbowl Crater

National Memorial Cemetery of the Pacific

Paradise Cove Luau

**Kailua Kona, Hawaii**

Atlantis Submarine

Kohala Coast

Ka'upulehu,

Kona's Painted Church

Pu'uhonua o Honaunau

Royal Kona Coffee

Mauna Kea Summit

Keck Observatory,

Kona Joe Coffee Farm

Original Hawaiian Chocolate Factory

Kona Natural Soap Company

Kona Beach

**Lahaina (Maui), Hawaii**

The Brick Palace of Kamehameha I

The Baldwin Home

Waiola Church and Cemetery

505 Front Street

Hana.

Drums of the Pacific Luau

Haleakala Crater

Iao Valley

Maui Tropical Plantation

Kaanapali Sunset Luau

Maui Ocean Center

Hali'imaile Pineapple Plantation

Hali'imaile General Store

The Surfing Goat Dairy

Pukalani Country Club

**Types of Excursions on a Celebrity Cruise:**

Adventure

Culinary

Entertainment

Flightseeing

Golf

Sand & Sea

Sightseeing

Snorkel & SCUBA

Wilderness

**What to Expect on the Ship:**

Celebrity Life SMActivities

Restaurants & Cafes

Lounges, Bars & Clubs

Spa & Fitness

Casinos

Outstanding Service

Special Needs

Shops

Entertainment

Shore & Land Excursions

Celebrity Wine Experience

Youth Programs

Special Occasions

**Staterooms**

All staterooms include:

**Services**

Celebrity signature friendly, personalized service with a guest to staff ratio of nearly 2:1

Twice daily bed service (makeup and turndown)

Daily ice service in stainless steel ice buckets

Dining

24-hour complimentary room service

Amenities

Robe

Complimentary tote bag

Custom blended bath products (shampoo, conditioner and lotion), shower cap, cotton balls and cotton swabs

Water/wine glasses

Celebrity eXhale bedding featuring 100% cotton linens and plush duvet, pillows and custom premium mattresses

Hair dryer

Stateroom Features

Private mini-bar*

Additional charges apply.

**Suites**

Celebrity's spacious suites transform your vacation into a completely indulgent experience. Guests enjoy special privileges and an extensive list of extended amenities. These include European-style butler service.

**AquaClass®**

These veranda staterooms offer spa elements infused into the stateroom experience. They also include priority seating in the exclusive and chic specialty restaurant, Blu. These spa-inspired staterooms offer unlimited access to the AquaSpa® Relaxation Room (on Solstice Class only). Guests also have access to the Persian Garden as well as a host of other soothing extras.

**Concierge Class**

Designed for the traveler who settles in to veranda staterooms where little details make a big difference. Savor unexpected delights such as fresh flower arrangements, personalized stationery, and complimentary shoeshine service. The attention to detail will amaze you, even as you sleep on the perfect pillow you've selected from our pillow menu. If personalized Concierge service, priority check-in and early disembarkation appeal to you, Concierge Class is your choice.

## Veranda Staterooms

Veranda Staterooms are private sanctuaries where you'll enjoy both in and outdoor space. Guests relax in the spacious lounge or step outside to linger over morning coffee or wonder at evening sunsets.

## Ocean View Staterooms

Ocean view staterooms have large windows and a sitting area. There you can kick back and relax after a day that has been as busy or relaxing as you want it.

## Inside Staterooms

Stateroom with ample living space with a sofa and sitting area.

In short, a Celebrity cruise can help you enjoy the wonders of the Pacific Coast, Alaska and selected destinations on the western Canada coast.

## American Safari Cruise

888-862-8881

http://www.un-cruise.com/

The American Safari small ship Hawaiian cruises embark on smaller ships. These ships can visit bays islands missed by the larger cruise ships. Activities include snorkeling, night snorkeling, kayaking, paddle boarding, sailing, beachcombing, and skiff excursions. Passengers may include macadamia nut and plumeria farm visits as well as partake in local cultural events.

Lana'i. American Safari offers seven-day cruises.

**Destinations may include:**

Shipwreck Beach

Humpback National Marine Sanctuary

Olowalu

Moloka'i

Kaunakakai

Halawa Valley

Kealakekua Bay

Honomalino Bay

Opihihali

Ka'ena Point State Park

Wai'anae Harbor

**Boats used:**

**Wilderness Explorer**

The newly renovated seventy-six guest Wilderness Explorer lusts for action, adventure, and exploration. Its interior complements the outside and public and private spaces bristle with amenities. The ship offers a main lounge featuring a Douglas fir bar top, dining room, and ample space on deck for taking in the great outdoors.

Three accessible decks are fully equipped for comfort and action. Guests enjoy over-the-top views from the bow. On-deck sauna and fitness equipment and the EZ Dock launch platform makes getting in the water a cinch, even for a novice. Onboard are kayaks, stand-up paddleboards, inflatable skiffs, hiking poles and yoga mats. Passengers may use and a hydrophone for listening below surface.

**The three cabin categories aboard the Wilderness Explorer are:**

Trailblazer

Pathfinder

Explorer

These cabins provide single and double accommodation.

Common to all Wilderness Explorer cabins are:

Flat-screen TV/DVD; and iPod docking station.

76 guests

Thirty-eight cabins

Twenty-six crewmembers

186 feet in length

38 feet wide

Cruising speed of 11 knots

Built in 1976; renovated in 2012

Registered in United States

3:1 Guest-to-crew ratio


**Sunstone Tours & Cruises**

1-888-815-5428

http://www.sunstonetours.com/hawaii/index.asp

Sunstone Tours and Cruises offers small ship cruises on yahts. The smaller ships provide a more intimate experience that achieved on the larger ships. Explore remote coves and shoreline of Maui, Moloka'i and Lana'i. Go by foot, kayak, paddle boarding, sailboat, mountain bike and motor launch.

Smaller ships provide an intimate exploration of the Hawaiian islands. Visitors achieve a better cultural experience that the large ships cannot achieve. Cruise itineary may change due to weather and wildlife movements. The captains like to take advantage of spontaneous viewing opportunities. Sunstone Tour cruises

**Ships:**

**Wilderness Explorer**

Passengers: 76

Crew: 26

Cabins: 38

Length: 186 ft

Width: 38 ft

Cruising Speed: 10 knots

Registry: United States

**Safari Explorer**

Cabins: 17 dbl; 1 single

Guests: 36 - 40

Length: 145 ft

Width: 36 ft

Draft: 8.5 ft

Crew: 14

Built: 1998

Last refurbishment: 2008

Cruising speed: 101 knots

Registry: United States

**Possible Destinations of a Sunstone Tour:**

Ka'ena Point State Park

Wai'anae Harbor

Humpback National Marine Sanctuary

Maui

Molokini

Lahaina.

Munro Trail

Honomalino Bay

Opihihali

Kona Coast

Honomalino Bay

Kailua Town

Hale 'o' Lono Harbor

Mo'omomi Preserve

Kalaupapa Trail

Manele Bay

Laparuse Trail

Ka Lae

Black Sands Beach

Place of Refuge

Kealakekua Bay

Kohala Coast.

Holualoa

**Star of Honolulu**

808-983-7827

Toll Free 800-334-6191

http://www.starofhonolulu.com

The Star of Honolulu offers a variety of cruises that include:

Dinner Cruises

Dinner and Music Cruises

Dinner

Show Cruises

Wildlife Viewing Cruises

Fireworks Cruises

There are no overnight cruises, these ships have no overnight facilities. All  the ships are on Oahu.

Vessel Name: Star of Honolulu

Location: Oahu, Aloha Tower Marketplace, Pier 8

Street Address: 1 Aloha Tower Drive, Honolulu, HI 96813

Total Capacity: 1,500 passengers

Length: 232 feet

Width: 45 feet

Type: 4-deck tour vessel equipped with 3 types of stabilizers

"Outstanding Passenger Vessel Design" Winner

The Star of  Honolulu has two elevators, a 60-foot observation deck and four walk around decks. There is a dining room, three ballrooms and private lounge.

Vessel Name: Dolphin Star

Location: Oahu, Wai'anae Boat Harbor

Street Address: 85-371 Farrington Highway, Wai'anae, HI 96792

Total Capacity: 149 passengers

Length: 65 feet

Width: 25 feet

Type: 2-deck catamaran with EPA compliant main engines

This boat is on the western portion of Oahu. The ship is well equipped for dolphin watching with two walk around decks.

Vessel Name: Starlite:

Location: Oahu, Kewalo Basin

Street Address: Kewalo Basin

Total Capacity: 149 passengers

Length: 65 feet

Width: 28 feet

Type: 2-deck catamaran


**Tradewinds Sailing Charters**

USA Toll Free 888 401 1430

International +1 784 457 3407

http://www.trade-winds.com/

Tradewinds Sailing Charters operate in the Caribbean and at several locations in Central America. They also have cruises in the Mediterranean and Ionian Seas. Voyages are also offered in the Canary Islands in the Atlantic Ocean as well. Operations also now include the Pacific Ocean in the Las Perlas Archipelago.

TradeWinds currently operates cruising bases in:

British Virgin Islands

St. Maarten

Antigua

Guadeloupe

St. Vincent

Grenadines

Tobago

Panama

Belize

Canary Islands

Greece

Turkey


**Wild Side Specialty Tours**

Oahu Hawaii

Waianae Boat Harbor

Kewalo Basin Harbor

(808) 306-7273

http://sailhawaii.com/index.html

Wild Side Specialty Tours offers half day, full day and multiple day tours. These are primarily wild life tours that focus on the wild areas of Hawaii. These cruises have reputations as providing excellent whale watching, snorkeling, dolphin and turtle encounters. Some of the cruises are inter-island.

**Destinations:**

Molokai

Lanai

Maui

Kauai

Niihau

Oahu

Cruise tour itineraries are flexible. The captains take advantage of wildlife viewing opportunities. Changing weather conditions and the whims of the passengers prevail.

The boats typically hold a six-passenger complement. There is a main salon with television, library, theater stereo system and juice bar. Passengers may bring alcohol. Topside aft is the location of an outdoor dining area with a gas barbeque grill. The compact passenger cabins have 110-volt outlets and individual air conditioner controls. The cruise line provides all meals on longer voyages. They use locally grown or caught foods as much as possible. Dress codes are lax, shorts, sarongs and swimsuits being the most common.

**Small Ships of Princess**

Small Ships of Princess offers a smaller complement of passengers. This allows the tourist a smaller, more intimate cruise experience. Small Ships of Princess currently offer an eleven-day and a twenty-seven day Hawaiian cruise. Both cruises entail visiting several Hawaiian ports of call as well as other South Sea Islands. These straight-line cruises begin and end in different ports.

**Currently there are two Small Ships of Princess:**

**Pacific Princess**

680 passengers

232 staterooms with private balconies (73 percent of all outside staterooms)

Two specialty restaurants, including Sabatini's Italian restaurant and Sterling Steakhouse

Poolside BBQ grill and pizzeria

24-hour dining and room service

A wide variety of bars and lounges

Swimming pool, includes two hot tubs

Lotus Spa, gym and fitness area

Golf practice cage, shuffleboard and jogging track

Casino

World-class art collection, gallery and auctions

Duty-free boutiques

24-hour Internet Cafe (wireless access avail)

Library and card room

**Ocean Princess**

680 passengers

232 staterooms with private balconies (73 percent of all outside staterooms)

Two specialty restaurants, including Sabatini's Italian restaurant and Sterling Steakhouse

Poolside BBQ grill and pizzeria

24-hour dining and room service

A wide variety of bars and lounges

Swimming pool, includes two hot tubs

Lotus Spa, gym and fitness area

Golf practice cage, shuffleboard and jogging track

Casino

World-class art collection, gallery and auctions

Duty-free boutiques

24-hour Internet Cafe (wireless access available)

Library and card room

**Ports Visited - Depending Upon Cruise Chosen:**

Hilo, Hawaii

Hawaii Volcanoes National Park

Tropical Botanical Gardens

Akaka or Rainbow Falls

Waipi'o Valley

Mauna Kea

Kealakekua Bay

Lava Tree State Park

Maui (Lahaina), Hawaii

Haleakala National Park

Maui Ocean Center

Road to Hana

Iao Valley State Park

Whale Watching

Molokini Crater

Kauai (Nawiliwili), Hawaii

Waimea Canyon

Wailua River & Fern Grotto

Na Pali Coast

North Shore of Kauai

Grove Farm Homestead

Kilaueau Lighthouse

Honolulu, Hawaii

Pearl Harbor & USS Arizona Memorial

Polynesian Cultural Center

Pali Lookout

Diamond Head Crater

Iolani Palace

Queen Emma Summer Palace

Hanauma Bay

Waimea Bay and North Shore

**Other Ports Visited - Depending Upon Cruise Chosen:**

Tahiti (Papeete),

French Polynesia

Moorea, Polynesia

Bora Bora, French Polynesia

Bora Bora, French Polynesia

Moorea, Polynesia

Tahiti (Papeete), French Polynesia

Pago Pago, American Samoa

Cross International Date Line

Apia, Western Samoa

Nuku'alofa, Tonga

Auckland, New Zealand

Tauranga, New Zealand | Sydney, Australia

**Tauck**

800-788-7885.

From the United Kingdom: 0800-961-834

From Australia: 1-800-122-048

From South Africa: 0800-990-476

From other countries: Contact Tauck in the U.S. at (203) 899-6500

http://www.tauck.com/

Tauck offers a single Hawaiian tour, a twelve-day tour of the four islands Maui, Kwaii, Oahu and the Big Island. This is a combination cruise and stays at resort hotels. The traveler enjoys oceanfront views from four fantastic Hawaiian hotels on four islands. There are free days for you to spend as you wish. The cruise line offers as planned excursions to allow the traveler to enjoy the Hawaiian experience as well. Passengers may extend the time before or after the cruise, if desired.

Cruise information from the Tauck website:

**Uncommon Access**

We take care of every detail on your cruise so you connect ashore with people, places, and cultural traditions

Shore excursions are a well-choreographed blend of cultural sightseeing and leisure time. This allows you to maximize your time.

Exclusive cultural experiences are an important part of Tauck's small ship cruising. Many of these are private for Tauck guests only

The price includes some meals ashore, providing a genuine taste of regional cuisine

**Included in the Cruise Price**

One upfront price covers almost all cruise expenses

No options sold

All shore excursions led by Tauck Directors and local guides

All gratuities to Tauck Directors, ship staff, local guides and luggage handling included

**Intimate, Club-like Atmosphere**

40-264 guests aboard Tauck's yachts and expeditionary vessels – comfortable, relaxed, personalized cruising

Cruise to small islands, hidden harbors and exclusive ports of call where big ships can't go

On-board presentations by local experts and cultural performances by local artists

**Peace of Mind**

Tauck's proven ability to take care of guests in the event of the unexpected on tour personifies the word "reassurance"

Cruise Protection Product offers trip, airfare, medical and luggage protection

Book your air with Tauck – taxes and fuel surcharges included, no hidden fees, refundable.

## Smithsonian Journeys

P.O. Box 23182

Washington, DC 20077-0843

855-330-1542

http://www.smithsonianjourneys.org/index.php

Smithsonian Journeys provides an educational experience to the traveler than most other cruise adventures. A study leader accompanies each tour group that is well versed in local customs and attractions. In addition, Smithsonian Journeys provides local speakers to impart their knowledge to the traveler. A professional tour manager also accompanies each tour. They handle the logistics of the group and to give morning briefings about what will be available on the tour that day. Smaller ships allow Smithsonian Journeys to penetrate into areas that the big ships cannot.

You do need to be a member of the Smithsonian Institute to be able to take part in these tours, but membership cost is minimal.

Smithsonian Journeys does not operate regular, scheduled cruises. Hawaiian cruises are not always available. Check the web site to find availability of a Hawaiian Cruise.

**Mossy Feet Books Catalog**

To Get Your Free Copy of the Mossy Feet Books Catalogue, go to www.mossyfeetbooks.com and click the catalogue link.

**Gardening Books**

*Abe's Guide to Growing the Tomato*

*The Solar Garden*

*Abe's Guide To The Peony*

*Abe's Guide to The Lanceleaf Coreopsis*

*Abe's Guide To The Threadleaf Coreopsis*

*Abe's Guide To The Creeping Phlox*

*Abe's Guide To The Hibiscus*

*Abe's Guide to Wall Germander*

*Abe's Guide To The Bearded Iris*

*Abe's Guide to the Chrysanthemum*

*Abe's Guide to the Fall Garden*

*Abe's Guide To Perennial Candytuft*

*Abe's Guide to Making Compost*

*Abe's Guide to Botany*

*Abe's Guide To Plant Stems*

*Abe's Guide to Buddleia*

*Abe's Guide to Leaves*

*Abe's Guide to Blanket Flower*

*Abe's Guide to Blackberry Lily*

*Abe's Guide to Flowers*

*Abe's Guide to Perennial Balloon Flower*

*Abe's Guide to Perennial Alyssum*

*Brilliant yellow blossoms and evergreen foliage make perennial alyssum a must for every perennial garden.*

*Abe's Guide to the Plant Root*

*The Complete Guide to the Plant Seeds*

*The Guide to Robotic Vacuum Cleaners*

*Abe's Guide to September/October Wildflowers*

*Abe's Guide to August Wildflowers*

*Abe's Guide to July Wildflowers*

*Abe's Guide to June Wildflowers*

*Abe's Guide to May Wildflowers*

*Abe's Guide to April Wildflowers*

*Abe's Guide to Growing Marigolds*

*Abe's Guide to Full Sun Perennials*

## Fantasy Books

*Fading Photographs*

*Calls After Midnight*

*The Pirate King*

*Bearl's First Test*

*Heir of the Pirate King*

*Rise of the Pirate King*

*Tarque's Search*

*The Fall of Acerland*

*Legend of the Wizard Tarque*

*Covenant's Peril*

*Tale of the Crystal Eye*

*Flea Market Tales – Collection 1*

*The Wine Goblet*

*Box of Secrets*

*Lament of Arii*

*Glade of Death*

*Before the Storm*

*Gault*

*The Order of Solaun*

*Radio Memories*

*Seven Day Clock*

*Revealed by the Light*

*Zerena*

*Restoration*

*Time of Troubles*

*War of the Crystal*

*The Oasis*

*Pillars of Borr*

*Turmoil*

*Awakening*

*Demon Soul*

*Barn of Fear*

*Ten Tales for the Campfire*

*Five Tales for the Campfire – Volume Two*

*Halloween Party*

*The Dinner Bell Rings at Midnight*

*The Sinkhole*

*The Woman in the Wind*

*Tale of the White Rock*

*Field of Snakes*

*What's in the Cooler, Mister?*

*The Covenant*

*Five Tales for the Campfire*

*Promise of the White Rock*

*The Skull Garden*

*The Hungry House*

*Appointment*

*The Rise of Gwaum*

*Pets*

*Footsteps*


**Gandy Rand – Erotic**

*Short Stories and Collections*

*Double Trouble*

*Motorcycle Ride*

*Mrs. Boswell*

*Sales Call*

*Slow Day*

*Five Erotic Stories Collection 1*

*Mile High Club*

*Euchre Game*

*Masquerade Ball*

*Candy Store*

*Special Delivery*

*Five Erotic Stories Collection 2*

*Five Erotic Stories Complete Collection*


**Humor Books**

*Stroke and Counterstroke*

*Five Stories From the Liar's Bench*

*Screams in the Night*

*Old Cameras Never Die*

*Whose Kidneys Are These, Anyway?*

*Practical Joke*

*Ad Space*

*Ten Funny Stories Complete Collection*

*Five Funny Stories – Volume II*

*Dog Ballooning*

*Holey Boat*

*Bring Your Pet to Work Day*

*An Ode to the Big Toe*

*Toe Tag*

*Five Funny Stories*

*Hole to China*

*One Fine Morning on Mulberry Lane*

*Perfect Afternoon*

*Truffle Shop Tale*

*The Adventures of Toby and Wilbur Complete Short Story Collection*

*Toby and Wilbur Bear– Legend of the Christmas Train*

*Toby and Wilbur and the Legend of the Trestletown Ghost*

*Toby and Wilber - The Great Kite Caper*

*Toby and Wilbur Bear – 3, 2, 1, Blastoff*

*Toby and Wilbur Bear – The Great Bear Race*

*Rich Woman's Dog*

*Bernie Fuller though life as a rich woman's dog would be a hoot.*

*Toby and Wilbur Bear – The Amazing Hovercraft Adventure*

*Toby and Wilbur – The Second Day*

*Toby and Wilbur – The Beginning Begins*


## Science Fiction Books

*Solar Power Primer*

*Alternative Energy Sources*

*Five Science Fiction Short Stories - Volume II*

*Ten Science Fiction Short Stories*

*Signals*

*Spores*

*Mind Games*

*Biology Experiment*

*The Database*

*Secretary General*

*Five Science Fiction Short Stories*

*Ad Campaign*

*The Smoke*

*The Elixir*

*Unacceptable Use of Resources*

*Down the Barrel of a Gun*


## Semi – Autobiographical Books

*Ten Ricky Huening Stories*

*Five Ricky Huening Stories – Collection II*

*1963*

*People Are Like Peanuts*

*Clay Rockets*

*Cookie*

*The Crick*

*Five Ricky Huening Stories – Collection I*

*Hauling Out the Trash*

*The Time Machine*

*The Chicken House*

*The Magic Swing*

*The Shoe Fence*


## Travel Books

*The Hawaiian Chronicles – Our Hawaiian Cruise Adventures*

*The Alaska Chronicles – Our Alaskan Cruise Adventure*

*Indiana State Park Series*

*A Visit to Pokagon State Park, Indiana*

*A Visit to the Falls of the Ohio*

*A Visit to the Land of Lincoln, Indiana*

*A Visit to Harmonie State Park, Indiana*

*A Visit to Brown County State Park*

*A Visit to Spring Mill State Park*

**History Books**

*American History A Day at A Time – July 2015 Edition*

*American History A Day at A Time – June 2015 Edition*

*American History A Day at A Time – May 2015 Edition*

*American History A Day at A Time – April 2015 Edition*

*American History A Day at A Time – March 2015 Edition*

*American History A Day at A Time – February 2015 Edition*

*American History A Day at A Time – January 2015 Edition*

*A Short History of the Game Of Chess*

*A Brief History of Candle Making*

*A Short History of Coins*

*A Short History of the United States Constitution*

*A Short History of Kites*

*A Short History of Transportation*

## Alaskan Vacation Cruise - Day One - Anchorage

The Alaskan cruise was several months in the planning, with help from my brother and his wife, who are travel agents. Once the cruise date was set it required several days planning the excursions we would take. There are several planned excursions available from the cruise line and we did take advantage of a couple of these. However, we like to see things at our on pace and on our own schedule. Therefore, I printed out maps and planned itineraries. I made rental car arrangements for the various ports on the internet.

Finally, travel day arrived! Arising very early, my sister in law was to take us to the airport. We showed up at her house around 5:00 AM and off to the airport we went! We checked in, whiled away the time reading until the plane started boarding. By 9:00 AM, we were in the air to Minneapolis on the first leg of our journey to the 49th state.

As the airplane descended through the clouds, the landscape of Minnesota became visible. It appears flat, the roads forming a pattern reminiscent of a tile floor. They were rectangles and squares of varying shades of green and brown. As we descended, the Mississippi River came into view. A train pulling multicolored cars was traversing tracks along the river. From our altitude, the train looked like a long beaded necklace as it moved along the pretty blue waters of the river. A lock on the river was visible and a barge was moving upriver.

We landed around 10:35 AM at Concourse G. I walked back to a food vendor to get lunch. We boarded the plane for Anchorage at 1:00 PM. We were in the air by 1:35 pm, just about one hour and forty-five minutes late.

This would be a rather long flight, about five hours. We passed the time reading and sleeping alternately. I had an aisle seat; my wife was across the aisle from me. I had a window seat, but I had surrendered it to a young lady traveling with her mother. I made the ladies' acquaintance and we engaged in conversation to help pass the time. They were from Montana, and were heading to Anchorage for a cruise, too. It was a gift from the daughter to her mother for her birthday. The young lady loaned me a National Geographic magazine about Alaska to read. We talked a bit about our home states and travels, among other things.

At 6:45 Indiana time, 3:45 PM Alaska time we landed in Anchorage, Alaska. We had caught brief glimpses of the Alaskan landscape through the clouds as we descended and what we saw was spectacular. The approach to Anchorage International Airport had taken us over Cook Inlet. Surrounding mountains were visible from the airport as we gathered our luggage. The cruise line representatives met us in the baggage claim area. They took our bags, loaded us on a bus and transported us to our hotel in downtown Anchorage.

Our trip was to consist of a three-day land tour. One day at Anchorage, two days at the Kenai Princess Lodge near Cooper Alaska in the Kenai Peninsula. We would stay tonight night at the Captain Cook Hotel in downtown Anchorage. We would travel by bus the next day, Saturday, August 27 to the Lodge. The land tour would precede a seven-day Voyage of The Glaciers along the Western coast of Alaska.

The cruise line representative deposited us in our room by 5:10 PM. All times for the duration of the trip will be in Alaska Time, which is three hours behind Indiana time. The hotel is first class. Our luggage had not arrived yet, so we decided to take a walk in Anchorage. The city is nice and the surrounding scenery is spectacular. The Knik Arm of the Cook Inlet's blue waters are visible to the west. The mountains of the Chugach National Forest were visible to the east. From Resolution Park, a couple of blocks east of our hotel, Mt McKinley would be visible to the north if not for a shroud of clouds. The park consists of an impressive wooden deck structure overlooking the inlet.

We walked to the nearby Glacier Brewhouse for dinner. I had a delicious Salmon BLT washed down with Amber Ale. Chocolate and caramel flavor this beer and it is simply delightful. My wife chose a shrimp and salmon Caesar salad.

We continued our walk along Anchorage's streets after dinner. The weather consisted of light rain showers interspersed with sunny skies. A rainbow became visible in the east above the city and mountains. We would observe another from our hotel window later in the evening.

The length of daylight was somewhat disconcerting. The sun was still shining brightly at 9:00 PM. It finally went down around 9:30 and it was daylight until 10:00. We finally went to bed around that time, having been up almost twenty-two hours.